746.92092
BER/BLA

Antonio Berardi

TAMSIN BLANCHARD

Antonio Berardi

Sex and Sensibility

Thames & Hudson

First published in the United Kingdom in 1999 by
Thames & Hudson Ltd, 181A High Holborn
London WC1V 7QX

© 1999 The Ivy Press

British Library Cataloguing-in-Publication Data
A catalogue record for this book is available from
the British Library

ISBN 0-500-01964-9

Printed and bound in Hong Kong
by Hong Kong Graphic Ltd

Contents

'No one said it would be easy. But creation is my life, pressure is my adrenaline and fashion is my drug. I've always been obsessed with experimenting, using the richness of yesteryear to create the dreams of tomorrow. My work is about perfection, fantasy, possibility, all within the confines of wearability. Working with some of the most innovative people in the world, the challenges are endless. They excite me and inspire me, feeding me with the desire to reach further. 'Never say never,' someone once said. Simple logic perhaps, but I have since only followed my dream. Family, friendships and fashion to me are everything, and I wouldn't have it any other way.'

Antonio Berardi

Introduction

FEBRUARY 1999, and Antonio Berardi is preparing for his first show away from London Fashion Week. For several seasons he has been threatening to take his show to Milan; this time, he has finally done it. Although he is a very British designer – his collections are packed with ideas and obscure references as only those of a Central St Martin's graduate can be – Antonio Berardi's parents are both Italian. Furthermore, like many other British designers, his backer and manufacturer are based in Italy.

The Italians are quick to embrace Berardi as their own. But for the first time since leaving college and setting up his business, Berardi has to prove himself. In London, designers are expected to be innovative and experimental. In Milan, the expectation is for something slick, professional and commercial. This time it is really serious: in effect, by showing in Milan, Berardi is moving himself and his business up a gear. The world – or the fashion world at least – is watching him with bated breath.

When Antonio Berardi graduated from St Martin's in June 1994, his name was already being talked about by the industry in London. Not only had he commissioned Manolo Blahnik, the ultimate shoemaker to the stars, to create his final collection shoes, but he had also left a tiny vial of his own perfume on the front-row

seats at his graduation show. From the beginning, he had a strong sense of who he was as a designer, what he was doing, and where he was going. He was not going to hang around. And with pieces from the graduation show selling to Liberty and the Knightsbridge designer store A La Mode, Berardi was in business.

Getting into St Martin's, however, was not easy. It took Berardi three tries but he refused to give up. 'I applied to St Martin's because I'd read about everyone who had been there and I wasn't interested in anywhere else. I got on the reserve list and I kept ringing but there were no places.' That summer he worked for his father's ice cream business, and went to Milan to find work in a studio. The following year he applied again, but was rejected. 'I was really devastated because I thought I'd worked really hard. I couldn't understand why,' he remembers. 'In the meantime, my sister Piera was working at John Galliano. There was a job going as production assistant and I got that. I applied again to St Martin's in February 1990, and this time got accepted. I went for an interview for the third time, and started working at John's that same day.'

By the time he began college, Berardi had been out in the working world for three years and had gained

Berardi's student sketchbooks from Central St Martin's reflect a passion for intricate cutting and fine detail.

Antonio Berardi's first commercial collection, for spring/summer 1996, featured hats by Philip Treacy and shoes by Manolo Blahnik.

considerable experience of the industry. The result of his relatively late start was a mature attitude from day one. There are elements of his graduation collection – the finely pleated skirt hems, the peaked shoulders, the pedal-pushers, the meticulously cut seam edgings, and the idea that things are not what they seem – that he is still exploring in his collections today. One only needs to flick through his college sketchbooks to see that the Berardi stamp was one hundred per cent there. His time at college had, in effect, been spent preparing not for his graduation, but for his début collection as a designer in his own right.

While at college, Berardi continued working with Galliano. 'It was fantastic at John's – I learned everything there. I had complete insight because everything was made in the studio and you saw it from start to finish. In the beginning, I was measuring out fabric, finding zips and buttons, bagging, picking things up, doing quality control.' This was when Galliano was based on London's King's Road. When the designer moved to Paris, he asked Berardi to go too; he readily agreed. 'I took my third year out. I was just there to help out and would sit and sew. After that, I had to go back to college and see if I could do it. I knew that I had to try and fulfil my own destiny.' In the summer before his final year he also did

'I started from humble

beginnings and I like it

that way. I need to know

who I am and feel the

walls around me.'

stints working with Jasper Conran, Hyper Hyper and Paul Costelloe. 'You realized your place. I was a student and expected to be a student. I began to learn about the fashion industry. Working while studying was the best thing that I could possibly have done.'

The first collection

Just over a year after leaving college, Antonio Berardi showed his first collection at London Fashion Week. By now he had set up in business with his friend from college, Priyesh Shah, who acted as Berardi's in-house PR. There was no perfume this time, but the hats were designed by Philip Treacy and the shoes, once again, by Manolo Blahnik. He even managed to convince a celebrity to model for him – all-important in the game of generating headlines and publicity – in the form of the Australian pop star Kylie Minogue. Stella Tennant, Emma Balfour and Georgina Cooper modelled too. It was a small collection, but it was slickly presented and had serious impact.

'We got a bank loan. As well as Philip Treacy and Manolo, we had Sam McKnight for the hair, Mary Greenwell for make-up and Anya Hindmarch doing the bags.' It was a highly respected and

Spring/summer 1996: all Berardi's signatures of cut and style were in place, including an acute attention to detail and references as diverse as sportswear and club culture.

well-established team, a wise move for a new designer trying to make his mark. 'More than anything, I think people needed something new. My work was very different to what other young designers were doing. Mine was beaded and embroidered, while other people's were all techy and pointy and mean. That first collection was, and still is, very me.'

The venue was Six Hamilton Place, in the heart of Mayfair. The room was painted with rich red lacquer; it made the audience feel as though they had climbed into a jewellery box. Princess Julia, one of London's more uncompromising DJs, mixed the music live as the models took their turns down the short catwalk. The shoes were dangerously high and sexy, and of course the clothes bore the intricate and elaborate cutting, the sex appeal and the glamour for which Berardi is now celebrated. It was high fashion for women who have no doubts about their sex appeal and the empowerment that it can give. 'Here at last was a happening,' enthused Alison Veness, fashion editor of the *Evening Standard*. 'There were tantrums, tears and not everyone got in. Antonio Berardi was the hot ticket of London Fashion Week.' In the *Independent*, Marion Hume wrote: 'Here were ideas fizzing with passion, commitment and drive.' Berardi was just 26, and he had arrived.

Fashion's new breed

Antonio Berardi's career kicked off at a time when British fashion was undergoing a major resurgence. Alexander McQueen, Hussein Chalayan, Clements Ribeiro, Sonja Nuttall and Fabio Piras had all graduated from St Martin's before him and with his first collections he quickly became part of the new breed of designers that the rest of the world was watching. Matthew Williamson, Anthony Symonds and Robert Cary Williams were in Berardi's year at St Martin's, and Julien MacDonald graduated from Brighton at the same time. For his second collection, Berardi was awarded sponsorship from the Marks & Spencer New Generation scheme and showed at the British Fashion Council tents outside the Natural History Museum. It was the only time he would show in such a sterile environment. For him, a fashion show is about drama and atmosphere. By collection three, he had managed to get sponsorship from Courvoisier and scraped together enough money to hire the Crush Bar at the Royal Opera House. It was a grand affair, with clothes to match the sweeping gilt staircase and the red plush velvet.

This was the season when the talent scouts for the French luxury goods group LVMH were in London in search of a designer to take over the reigns of the House of Givenchy, following John

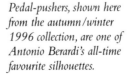

Beautifully cut tailoring was a feature of Berardi's second show. Honor Fraser wears a buttery yellow tunic with a detached collar.

'I like strong women. I think my clothes empower women. They don't make them feel vulnerable, but powerful and sexy.'

Pedal-pushers, shown here from the autumn/winter 1996 collection, are one of Antonio Berardi's all-time favourite silhouettes.

Galliano's promotion to the more lucrative and prestigious Dior. They chose the more controversial – and more established – British designer, Alexander McQueen. But for a young designer such as Berardi, who was only just into his third collection, it was quite something to have LVMH scouts seated front row at his show. And of all his collections, perhaps this was the one that delivered purest essence of Berardi.

The reference points were wide-ranging and numerous, all thrown into the Berardi blender and whizzed around a few times until a unique mix of religion, boxing, Aubrey Beardsley, football, sex, childhood innocence, drama, seduction and – in true Sicilian style – corruption poured out onto the catwalk. There was a hat made of playing cards, impossibly fanned above the model's head as though they had just been shuffled in the flick of a hand. There were knuckle-duster rings, lots of them, made out of Lalique glass; there were graffiti-sprayed jackets, referring to the street and club culture Berardi knows so well; there were dandyish pedal-pushers finished with a Regency bow at the calf; and there was a tightly laced corset, a showpiece designed by Berardi and created by the corsetier who also works

Epitomizing the spring/summer 1997 collection, a fragile organza dress is teamed with a boxer's belt and a hat made of Sicilian playing cards.

The spring/summer 1997 collection mixed a multitude of references. The spray-graffiti Slag jacket, left, was a typically raw and humorous touch from the street.

with Christian Lacroix and John Galliano, Mr Pearl. It was a self-assured, no-holds-barred extravaganza that said, 'Look at me. Look at the ideas, the reference points and the technical brilliance. Look at what I am capable of.'

The LVMH representatives were impressed by what they saw and invited Berardi to Paris to talk about his work. As well as the Givenchy job, the company was looking for innovative designers to generate publicity for Céline and Louis Vuitton. For a few seasons, he was mentioned in connection with jobs at almost every fashion house in Milan, including Versace; he was also offered a licensing deal that involved selling his name. Although it meant he would have to struggle financially, Berardi turned down offers. 'The name is not for sale,' he says. 'Once you sell that, you lose control.'

Despite all the talk and hype, Antonio Berardi was still a young designer and a fledgling business. After the Crush Bar show came the 'Voodoo' collection at the Camden Roundhouse. With an injection of cash from his newly signed Italian backers, Givuesse, this was Berardi's first fully-fledged, full-sized collection. With 60 outfits on the catwalk and still more on the rails in the showroom, the collection became a commercially viable proposition, attracting 55 stockists worldwide.

'Voodoo' was a turning point for Berardi. No longer was he a small independent designer, struggling to make ends meet and to find ways to finance the production of each collection. From that point on he was allowed to concentrate on research and design, on sourcing new techniques and refining his ideas. He managed to make a collection that was packed with new ideas, innovative cutting and radical styling, but that was also commercial. 'I am a romantic,' he declares, 'but I am a realist too.' By the fifth collection – a bright and bold affair at the Brixton Academy which gave Berardi the opportunity to put his name in lights and mixed elements of Sicily, New York, Miami and Las Vegas – his stockist list had grown to over one hundred.

Early influences

The clothes and the showmanship speak for themselves, but it would not be a Berardi show without a strong element of his family being present. Family ties are extremely important for the designer. They keep his feet on the ground. He has shared a flat with his sister since moving to London and likes to return home to his parents in Lincolnshire after

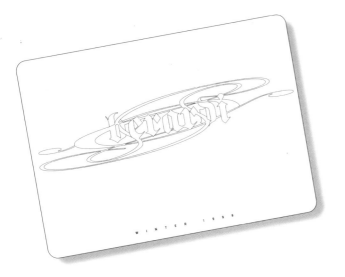

For the autumn/winter 1998 show (above and left), Berardi mixed street style and couture techniques. Right: Stella Tennant models a mini zig-zag pleated skirt and jacket for spring/summer 1998.

every collection. 'We've always been a very close-knit Sicilian family,' he says. 'I had a very Italian upbringing. I started from humble beginnings and I like it that way. I need to know who I am and feel the walls around me.'

Although they originally wanted him to become a doctor or lawyer, Berardi's parents have been supportive of their son's chosen career. 'Like all immigrant parents, mine wanted for me what they never had. They wanted us to have an education and go on to better things.' When his father moved to England at the age of 16, he worked as a miner. Berardi could not have found a more fantastical jump if he had tried. But right from Berardi's first collection, his father was convinced that his son was doing the right thing.

His mother and older sister are strong influences on him. 'Piera is my greatest supporter,' he says. 'She is also my severest critic. If she thinks something is awful and no one will wear it, she's not afraid to say so. She is the most stylish woman I know. My mother, Concettina, is 65 and still beautiful.' The women in his family rule the roost. 'I like strong women,' he says. 'I think my clothes empower women. They don't make them feel vulnerable, but powerful and sexy.' And that, more than anything, is the essence of Antonio Berardi and the key to understanding the designer and his work.

'I grew up around my grandmother and aunts embroidering constantly,' says Berardi. Although his mother didn't make clothes, there was always a strong sense of pride in what the family was wearing. 'There were times when my father brought me and my brother to London to have suits made. We always had to look well dressed. We were always smart, always had shoes to match.' Berardi is the youngest of five. His sisters were teenagers while he was still a child and, he says, 'I would get musical influences from them, and from the people who worked with my father – they were all into Tamla Motown and northern soul. It was pre-punk, the mid-1970s. I still like that music, anything with rhythm to it, including disco.'

Not surprisingly, the young Berardi was acutely aware of his clothes. 'I was conscious of labels because I went to Italy. The first thing I remember spending a fortune on was an Armani sweater that had gussets on the shoulders, and leather – it was fantastic, the most amazing thing I ever had.' He would avidly read *i-D* and the *Face* when they were first launched, and study the clothes and the designers who made them. 'I had clothes by Gaultier, John Flett, Katharine Hamnett. You name it, I had it, and I had to have it. It was all so alien to my contemporaries at school who didn't know what I was on about. But that was my introduction to fashion.'

'I like to make a woman into an icon in terms of strength. It is a very Mediterranean attitude.'

Classic cutting and unorthodox fabrics are combined in this coloured raffia jacket with asymmetric skirt, spring/summer 1999.

Berardi commissioned this fabric to be woven specially for the 'Voodoo' collection, autumn/winter 1997.

13

The Berardi aesthetic is very Italian. It is about dressing up and showing off. It is about making women look beautiful. And there is nothing wrong with a bit of sex appeal. Compared to many of his contemporaries, Berardi's attitudes towards dressing women are strangely old-fashioned. It is undoubtedly an attitude that has been bred in him since childhood, a cultural identity whereby men look like men, and women look like women. 'In my heritage, women are the people who mould your mind. I don't like women to be vulnerable. I like to make a woman into an icon in terms of strength. It is a very Mediterranean attitude.'

These days, it is Berardi's work that appears in the pages of the *Face* and *i-D*, and his clothes that readers look at and want to buy. But Berardi knows that a designer is only the Next Big Thing for a short period of time, and that to have long-term success it is necessary to move on. 'I never want people to want Berardi just because it's the label to buy. I don't want to be a flash in the pan.' He is, however, determined to set his own trends, define his own silhouettes and follow his own agenda. 'To me it's really personal. I was once asked whether I go and look on the high street. But why would I want to do that? To know what everybody else is wearing? That's not what I'm about. That's not what a designer

does. At least it's not what this designer does.' He wants his clothes to be relevant for more than a single season. 'Gone are the days when you bought clothes and it was seasonal. People buy clothes now because they like them. That's the most important thing.' And he is right: fashion is no longer so much about wearing a specific trend at a specific moment in time. Consumer patterns have changed and the discerning designer-clothing buyer is more interested in owning a piece that is in some way special – hand-finished, or made out of a unique material – than buying a label for its own sake. 'I want somebody to go into a shop and be dazzled and say, "I have to have that."'

As with any good designer, Berardi's talent is in knowing what the consumer wants before they know it themselves. By moving his show to Milan, he was able to place that instinctive London cutting edge within an atmosphere much more conducive to serious business. It was a gamble, but the Italian fashion industry welcomed him with open arms. For Antonio Berardi, 'Never Mind the Borgias', the collection for autumn/winter 1999, was a passport into the new millennium.

'Never Mind the Borgias': Nicholas Jurnjack designed dramatic hair pieces for the models, who included Kirsty Hume (above). The clothes were Berardi's most ambitious to date.

The punk-inspired invitation to the autumn/winter 1999 show.

Stephen Jones' hat designs for 'Never Mind the Borgias' included a series of extravagant creations based on nuns' wimples. The full-length coat and dress were hand-painted with specially commissioned designs.

'The name is not for sale.

Once you sell that, you

lose control.'

15

Glamour and sex appeal

'TO ME, GLAMOUR is about anything from the way you do your hair to the perfume you wear.' Antonio Berardi's clothes are for women who make that little bit of extra effort. They are not Oscars dresses – he doesn't design the shiny sheath dress or the slinky slip that Hollywood movie stars love to wear. He has, however, redefined glamour for the 1990s. It might be Meg Mathews in a leather trouser suit, or a New York clubber in a denim dress with a stripe of pink Swarovski crystals across it. For Berardi, glamour has an edge: it says 'Look, but don't you dare touch.'

According to Berardi, glamour is hard to define. 'I don't think that putting on a really expensive frock makes you glamorous. When a woman puts perfume behind her knees, that's glamorous. A denim jacket can be glamorous, but it depends on how you wear it.' Whatever it is, Antonio Berardi undoubtedly makes clothes for women who want to look one hundred per cent female. There are no two ways about it: a Berardi dress oozes sex appeal from its very seams. His is, of course, a very Mediterranean sensibility.

When Kylie Minogue stepped onto the catwalk for Berardi's first collection, in September 1995, she did so in a red dress that looked as though it was a second skin, with little flutes of chiffon trailing away from the

ESTHER CANADES
Autumn/winter 1997

The Spanish model is strong, sexy and untouchable – traits which are typical of the 'Berardi woman'.

CHRYSTELLE
Spring/summer 1997

A show-stopping hat by Stephen Jones counterbalances a black chiffon dress that shows Berardi at his most delicate and feminine.

KYLIE MINOGUE
Spring/summer 1996

Kylie's celebrity status added to the hype and thrill of Berardi's debut show. The star's barely-there red dress made newspaper headlines the next day.

DIAPHANOUS DRESSES
Spring/summer 1997

These delicate chiffon and organza dresses draw on lingerie-making techniques rather than traditional dressmaking. The spaghetti straps are so fine they might have been spun from air.

SPUN CASHMERE DRESS
Spring/summer 1999

A more subtle approach to sexy dressing: the hem of this fine cashmere dress is crocheted to add to its delicate, fragile appeal.

body and spaghetti straps so fine they looked as though they would snap. Kylie looked sensational and caught the newspaper headlines the next morning. The appeal of wearing a Berardi dress is that it will get you noticed. The more camera flashes the better. 'I'd been making clothes for Kylie already,' recalls Berardi. 'Up until that point, had you ever seen a pop star on the catwalk? Kylie wore that same dress on an awards show a year later, which made me really happy.'

Berardi aims to design clothes that enhance the wearer's femininity. 'I design clothes to make women look beautiful and sexy,' he says. But ultimately, he admits his clothes are only as sexy as the wearer. 'A genuinely sexy woman can come in all sorts of shapes and sizes and would look good in a bin liner. It's not what you wear that matters, but the signals you give off. I want my clothes to empower women.'

CROPPED JACKET
Spring/summer 1997

Typically sexy, this plunge-necked cropped jacket is also an example of Berardi's cutting at its most innovative.

TANGO DRESS
Spring/summer 1998

Inspired by Latin dancing and hot Miami nights, this multilayered dress was an integral piece in the Brixton Academy show.

19

ASYMMETRIC CHIFFON DRESS
Autumn/winter 1997

Berardi wanted this dress, worn by Emma Balfour, to look like the remains of something more substantial – a 'piece of nothing'. He hand-shanked the shoulder so that it would appear to be coming apart.

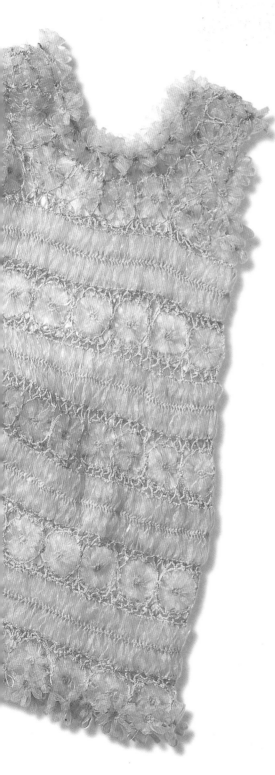

To wear Berardi's clothes, you need a certain amount of attitude. Michelle Hicks, the American model, is the epitome of Berardi's 'I'm too sexy for you, don't even think about it' tough girl spirit. 'She's like a predator. There's something feline about her. I love the way she stalks the catwalk, I love her attitude.' Hicks is sexy, but she is also hard and strong. Berardi often uses this mix of the hard and soft in his collections. 'I like the idea of woman as predator, woman competing with man, the idea that woman is stronger than man. I hate to see women as vulnerable. I think most of the women I know who wear my clothes feel good in them and strong in them. They know they'll get attention, but in a good way.'

Berardi's ideal woman is as curvaceous as Sophia Loren after a bowl of spaghetti. 'That's so much more feminine and beautiful than when you see stick-thin women. My silhouette has always been based on a woman's natural body. I simply embellish it.' Despite the skinny models who wear the clothes on the catwalk, Berardi insists he designs for 'the womanly figure'. 'For the show you make the clothes to fit the models. But the proportions of my clothes are for the kind of woman I like. The Mediterranean woman is what I grew up with – it was like learning to speak. It was just there.'

CROCHET
DRESS
Spring/summer 1998

Michelle Hicks, one of Berardi's favourite models, wears a hand-crocheted dress on the catwalk at Brixton Academy. Made from 3mm-wide organza ribbon, the entire dress was elasticated so that it stretched over the body, leaving little to the imagination.

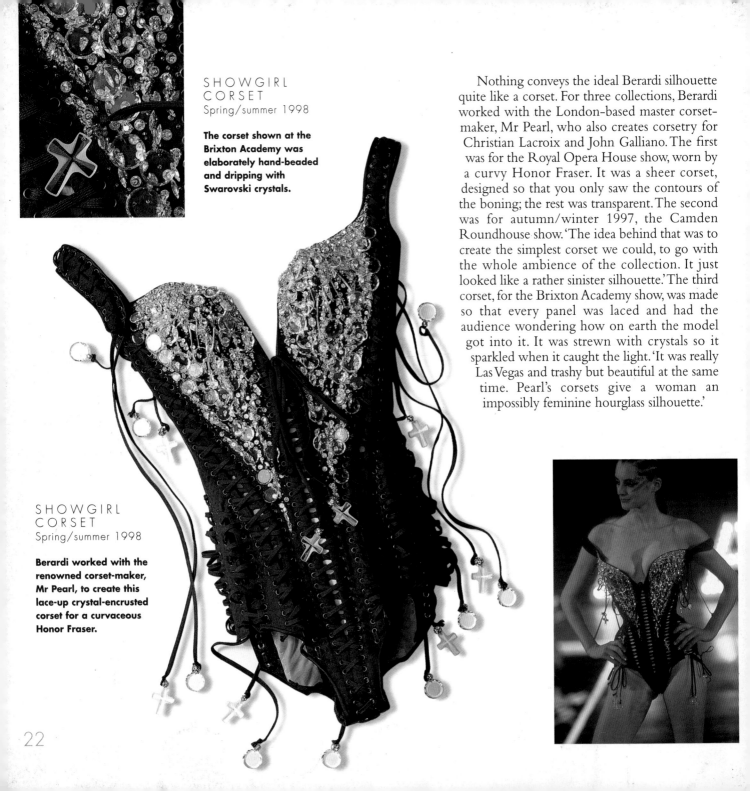

SHOWGIRL
CORSET
Spring/summer 1998

**The corset shown at the
Brixton Academy was
elaborately hand-beaded
and dripping with
Swarovski crystals.**

SHOWGIRL
CORSET
Spring/summer 1998

**Berardi worked with the
renowned corset-maker,
Mr Pearl, to create this
lace-up crystal-encrusted
corset for a curvaceous
Honor Fraser.**

Nothing conveys the ideal Berardi silhouette
quite like a corset. For three collections, Berardi
worked with the London-based master corset-
maker, Mr Pearl, who also creates corsetry for
Christian Lacroix and John Galliano. The first
was for the Royal Opera House show, worn by
a curvy Honor Fraser. It was a sheer corset,
designed so that you only saw the contours of
the boning; the rest was transparent. The second
was for autumn/winter 1997, the Camden
Roundhouse show. 'The idea behind that was to
create the simplest corset we could, to go with
the whole ambience of the collection. It just
looked like a rather sinister silhouette.' The third
corset, for the Brixton Academy show, was made
so that every panel was laced and had the
audience wondering how on earth the model
got into it. It was strewn with crystals so it
sparkled when it caught the light. 'It was really
Las Vegas and trashy but beautiful at the same
time. Pearl's corsets give a woman an
impossibly feminine hourglass silhouette.'

SHEER CORSET
Spring/summer 1997

Also worn by Honor Fraser, this was the first corset designed by Berardi in conjunction with Mr Pearl. In girly pink, it is boned and structured to draw attention to the model's breasts and hips and to give her an impossibly small waist. Berardi declares that he prefers voluptuous figures to skinny, boyish ones.

BLACK CORSET
Autumn/winter 1997

Here Berardi wanted to strip a corset to its essentials, making a pure but 'rather sinister' silhouette.

VEGAS COWGIRL
Spring/summer 1998

Kate Moss loved this outfit: stetson by Stephen Jones, micro dress, and Manolo Blahnik kinky boots.

Two Berardi trademarks are high heels and short skirts. Berardi argues that his clothes are meant to empower women but this is the sort of thing that drives feminists – even post-feminists – to accuse him of misogyny. 'Unfortunately, we still live in a society where a woman wearing a short skirt is thought to be sending off certain signals. There is nothing anti-women in my collections, nothing that would make women feel inadequate. What I do is really a celebration of women.' The key to his clothes is, if you don't like it, don't wear it. That also goes for high heels – which, admittedly, are not a practical proposition for many women. But from an aesthetic point of view, Berardi loves them. 'I like what heels do to the calf muscles and the way they define the leg. They not only alter your posture but can change your whole attitude.'

Everything is about balance and harmony. A pair of high heels will balance a particular dress or skirt. 'There are certain rules,' says Berardi. 'You play down the top because the short skirt is the emphasis. If we do a short skirt, we'll juxtapose it with something long. The short skirt can set a proportion, especially on the catwalk.' And off the catwalk, when a skirt goes into production, it will be made a few inches longer. 'A lot of things are exaggerated for the catwalk in order to get a message across. It's just like a fashion illustration: if you draw it in proportion, then it won't have nearly so much impact.'

HIGH-HEELED MULES
Autumn/winter 1997

Since his graduation collection from Central St Martin's, Berardi has worked with celebrity shoe designer Manolo Blahnik to create impossibly sexy shoes. The tough mules give an edge to the fluid, feminine floaty skirt.

Art and craft

IT BECAME KNOWN as the 'wow dress'. 'Wow' because when Naomi Campbell stepped out into the camera flashes at Berardi's spring/summer 1998 collection at the Brixton Academy, wearing a white lace second-skin outfit, she looked sensational. 'Wow' because she had to be sewn into it – and cut out of it again – backstage. And 'Wow' because the dress took 14 Italian lacemakers four months to make. It was hard to put a price on such a garment – indeed it was given to Berardi as a gift from the Mayor of Offida, where lacemaking is an ancient tradition. 'Only one shop in Japan bought the dress, but it was important to do. It was historical – it was the first bobbin-lace dress they'd ever made. They only usually use it for small details like collars.'

Antonio Berardi's work is as much about details as it is about trends and ideas. While the catwalk is a great vehicle to display the designer's collections and to generate excitement among the press, it only allows a superficial look at the clothes. And the real essence of Berardi is in the embroidery, the finishing of a seam, the cut work on a leather jacket or the intricacy of a lace dress. Much of his work is hand-finished, sometimes completely hand-made, and part of his mission in life is to keep alive the work of some of the fine craftspeople around Italy. 'I always try something new. I might pleat chiffon and embroider on top of it, so it looks like gothic script. Or I might decide I want to use traditional

BOBBIN-LACE
DRESS
Spring/summer 1998

Offida has a long tradition of lacemaking (*above left*). It took 14 women four months to make this sensational dress.

SHEEPSKIN
JACKET
Autumn/winter 1998

**The softest sheepskin is
hand-embroidered to
make it even more special.**

Capo di Monte porcelain for a head-dress. My work is more about particular touches than having a garment that is a particular shape or structure. That's what inspires me more.'

Berardi has a special talent for seeking out a particular craft and finding a way of making it new, modern and his own. But it is time-consuming and painstaking work. 'I make it my business to go and see every craftsperson I work with and to get to know them. It is really important because they have to believe in what I believe in, and understand what it is I want.' So his time in Italy is spent on trains, in cars and on planes, travelling the length and breadth of the country, tracking down small artisans, lacemakers, glass-blowers, embroiderers, beaders and specialist fabric mills. 'It's all about the attention to detail,' he says. 'Even a simple T-shirt will have some kind of technique. I can't give you boring.'

For spring/summer 1999, Berardi decided he wanted a wooden handbag, so his assistant in Italy found him a woodcarver. 'He looked like St Joseph,' says Berardi, who went to meet him to explain the idea. 'He thought I was insane, but I talked to him until he believed in it and he made it work. It's always like that. They get excited by the world of fashion, but they think you're mad.' And so, the carved wooden handbag – which appeared on the catwalk for all of 30 fleeting seconds – was made, intricate in its details and delicately hinged. Pieces like these are never put into production. They are one-offs, but for Berardi, nothing is too much trouble. Without the wooden

WOODEN
ACCESSORIES
Spring/summer 1998

**For the Student Prince
collection, Berardi
commissioned
woodworkers to craft
oversized bangles and a
handbag intricately
carved out of solid wood.
The bag is hinged along
the bottom.**

27

GOLD SHOES
Spring/summer 1999

A model is fitted with 18-carat gold shoes before the show. Outrageously expensive, they were escorted to the venue by personal guard.

CAPO DI MONTE HEADPIECE
Spring/summer 1999

Berardi set himself and milliner Stephen Jones an almost impossible task: to create hats from traditional Capo di Monte porcelain. When the headpieces arrived in London, some were broken and others were not as fragile and fine as the designers had envisaged. But a couple survived, including this gravity-defying bow.

VENETIAN GLASS CLOG
Spring/summer 1998

The delicate Venetian glass tinkling on these wooden clogs is a work of art in itself. Berardi spent time and energy tracking down glass-blowers, who made every piece for the shoes and accompanying headpieces by hand.

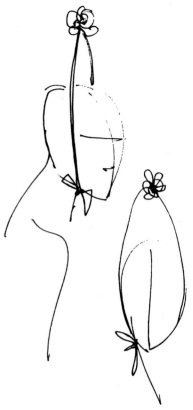

FINISHING TOUCHES
Spring/summer 1997

An enormous amount of thought and energy goes into creating elements that will only be seen once on the catwalk. Face jewellery added a touch of the exotic for the Royal Opera House collection, while the headpieces were among Stephen Jones' most charming and witty creations. Above: original sketches by Stephen Jones.

29

WICKER SKIRT
Spring/summer 1999

Constantly in search of new ways to adapt traditional crafts, Berardi used wickerwork to create a skirt and basket-style wicker corset. The bolero top is woven from raffia.

BOBBIN-LACE DRESS
Autumn/winter 1999

Berardi's second bobbin-lace dress was no less complex than the first. This time he commissioned it in black, which proved difficult for the lacemakers who worked on it during the short winter days. Suspended from fine threads in the fullness of the skirt are several tiny butterflies, also made of bobbin lace.

bag, or the heavy wooden bangles from the same collection, the show would not – in Berardi's mind at least – be complete.

As Berardi spends time between New York, Rimini (his Italian base) and London, he relies on his Italian assistant, Alfredo, to put him in touch with the right artisan or craftsperson in Italy. 'He is my eyes and my ears out there. He will drive up and down the country until he finds what I am looking for. For the autumn/winter 1999 collection, Alfie has been to the Vatican Museum in Rome; to Verona, Vicenza and Milan; to various laboratories and embroiderers; to see a woman in Florence who crochets straw; and to meet print people in Como.'

Berardi thrives on solving difficult problems and making the apparently impossible, possible. 'Everything is possible. Half the battle is finding the right person, and the other half is convincing them to do it. I do love a problem.' And the collections are always full of elements that are not what they seem, or pieces that make onlookers wonder, 'How did he do that?' For the spring/summer 1998 collection, for instance, he covered shoes with flowers blown from Venetian glass. 'I liked the idea of cheap Sicilian clogs, but wanted them to be fragile as well. We had them made in Murano, near Venice. They tinkled when you walked and there was something magical about them.' For autumn/winter 1998 he found a way to do delicate embroidery on sheepskin, and for spring/summer 1999 he worked with Manolo Blahnik to make shoes out of 18-carat gold. For the autumn/winter 1999 collection he returned to the bobbin-lacemakers for another dress. This time the lace was black – which was even more of a challenge for the lacemakers, being harder to see while being made on dark winter afternoons. But Berardi is no less demanding: 'It's huge: it comes down to the floor with a really high neck. The edges all look like fine net, but they are actually still made from bobbin lace.'

LEATHER JACKET
Autumn/winter 1997

This design was a challenge because each diamond-shaped cut-out was hand-finished – a process that proved very laborious and expensive. Nevertheless, it was one of the best sellers of the season.

MOIRE PRINT SHEEPSKIN DRESS
Autumn/winter 1999

This long body-hugging dress was printed with a moire design on the exterior, and dyed acid green inside. The sheepskin was then slashed to add texture.

EXPERIMENTS IN LEATHER
Autumn/winter 1996
Autumn/winter 1997

Crafted in a multitude of ways, leather has appeared regularly on the Berardi catwalk. A fitted snakeskin jacket is given appliqué detailing in an early collection. For the 'Voodoo' collection (*below right*) Berardi pieced together chevrons, in racing-driver style, and shredded kid leather to give a more dramatic, romantic feel.

**Leather becomes the canvas for
an intricate flower painting,
done by hand in Italy.**

There are times, however, when even Berardi wonders at the lengths to which he will go for a special piece which will usually never see the light of day once a collection is over. 'You experiment with new things and you think, I killed myself to get that wicker corset and jacket, and at the end of the day people don't care.' But ultimately the craft pieces are important to put across a certain message. Akin to haute couture, they represent the pure, uncompromising essence of a collection.

This labour of love does not just apply to showpieces. The most expensive piece of the spring/summer 1999 collection was a hand-painted leather trouser suit; each jacket took 60 hours to paint. In the autumn/winter 1999 collection one of the key pieces was a sheepskin dress, slashed and red-printed like moire around the outside, with tiny acid green curls on the inside. Skin-tight in the usual Berardi style, its

33

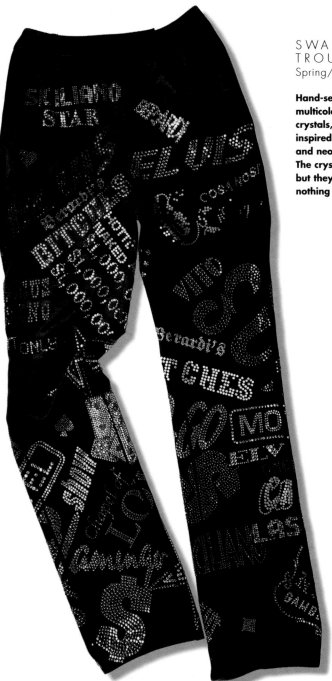

SWAROVSKI TROUSERS
Spring/summer 1998

Hand-sewn with multicoloured Swarovski crystals, these trousers were inspired by the bright lights and neon signs of Las Vegas. The crystals are expensive, but they pick up the light like nothing else.

appearance on the catwalk belied the complex layers of construction it had gone through. 'We had to get one side dyed red and one side green, which was a problem to get right. Then it had to be sent to one company that etched the moire design into it, and then another company where they slashed it. On the catwalk, you see a finished product and it's a sheepskin dress. You'd never believe the process it has to go through. Rather than being really obvious and in-your-face, it's a much more delicate way of seeing something. People will never appreciate that from a catwalk show, but that's life.' Ultimately, it is worthwhile for the customer who understands the workmanship that has gone into a garment. And Berardi wouldn't have it any other way. 'Nothing is simple for me,' he admits. 'Nothing.'

SWAROVSKI JACKET
Spring/summer 1998

Model Stella Tennant wore the trousers (*left*) with this matching sparkly jacket for the Brixton Academy show.

STRETCH CASHMERE TROUSERS
Autumn/winter 1998

Narrow-leg trousers are trimmed with Tyrolean-style silk braiding – a finishing touch that is very Berardi.

PLEATED SUIT
Autumn/winter 1998

Attention to detail: a classic suit is made special by using finely pleated fabric, trimmed with embroidered braid and given a serrated edge.

GANGSTER COAT
Autumn/winter 1998

Subtle satin edging around the lapels and pockets is developed into a hand-finished hem detail.

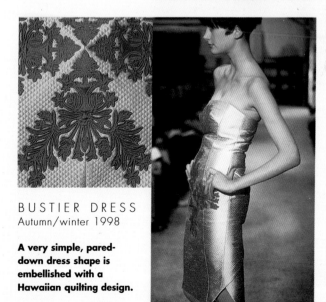

BUSTIER DRESS
Autumn/winter 1998

A very simple, pared-down dress shape is embellished with a Hawaiian quilting design.

Inspirations and influences

'**N**OTHING IS BEYOND my realms or my reach. Sometimes I think it might be interesting for somebody to say to me, "Here's three things – go and make a collection," because you can, if you put your mind to it.' Antonio Berardi is a master of research: behind every collection there is not only an idea, but also a whole body of information – both written and visual – which is crucial to the design process. Ultimately, however, he believes a collection should be 'about a feeling, an emotion, something that triggers off the imagination. You shouldn't have to write a thesis about it.'

A handful of recurring themes underlie Berardi's work: religion, Sicilian culture, club culture, sportswear. Looking through sketchbooks from his days at Central St Martin's, one can see the triggers that would later form the foundations for a collection. His graduation collection took its theme from Sicily: 'It was based on the Count of Cagliostro, who was a Sicilian peasant and confidence trickster.' Things were not what they seemed: 'With a jacket, you'd wear the lining and the jacket would appear to be hanging off your shoulder. I had double linings and money sewn in between layers of organza. It reminded me of

STUDENT
SKETCHBOOKS
Central St Martin's, 1991–92

Found images, texts and sketches from Berardi's second-year sketchbook show the beginnings of the designer's process of research and development. Ideas books such as these were encouraged by the tutors at Central St Martin's.

'DO OR DIE' DRESS
Spring/summer 1997

The gothic-script motif on this dress was inspired by an LA gang member's tattoo, while the neckline is based on the Nike 'swoosh'. The 'noose' earring is a response to the controversy about 'heroin chic' models.

going to Sicily as a kid, when Mum would pin
money into our underpants because you couldn't
take much cash into the country.' Fiction thus
becomes fashion, which in turn reflects events in
Berardi's own life.

The starting point for every collection is a
scrapbook which Berardi fills with visual imagery
that might spark an idea for a shoulder, a design
for lace, a reference for a hairstyle, or a detail for
a hat. The Royal Opera House book includes
pages of Aubrey Beardsley drawings alongside
pictures of old military uniforms, religious
iconography, boxers, Wallis Simpson, Victorian
bustles, 18th-century jackets, assorted underwear
and the Queen Mum. Looking through the pages
he stops at a picture of an old French woman
sewing gloves together. 'I loved the idea of a scarf
made of gloves; I love tailored things too: bustle-
back jackets, menswear, these are all just images
of things I like.' Another image features an LA
gang member with a tattoo in gothic script: 'That's
where we got the idea for the "Do or Die" logo.'

37

Berardi's skill is in combining these diverse references and ideas, and creating a coherent collection out of them. 'You shouldn't necessarily see the references in the final collection,' he says. 'A good designer can mix together several different references and the audience – and customer – will be unable to recognize the original research.'

First and foremost, however, Berardi is inspired by women: 'I've been surrounded by women all my life.' Berardi's notion of strong, powerful women influences everything he designs, from the Voodoo Bride to the warrior women in the 'Student Prince' collection and Lucrezia Borgia for autumn/winter 1999. Often this meets the Sicilian theme head-on: he might take inspiration from the way his mother and grandmother used to dress, or from the Catholicism that was a key part

CHRIST JACKET
Spring/summer 1998

Religion, especially Catholicism, is a strong theme running through Berardi's work. This jacket is hand-painted with a mosaic-like image of Christ, reminiscent of those Berardi would have seen in the Sicilian churches he visited as a boy.

FLAME JACKET
Autumn/winter 1997

For the 'Voodoo' collection, the flames used in Brazilian macumba were represented both on the clothes and with real flames on the catwalk. The imagery was taken from customized Harley Davidsons and ZZ-Top spray art.

of any childhood visit to his parents' home. 'My memories of granny are of her saying her rosary while she was crocheting. Every summer we would go to Sicily and I would be immersed in Catholicism: there were marvellous statues, gold and white church interiors, and you'd hear stories about saints. It was very rich in imagery. There's something in Catholicism that I find very sensual – that whole pomp and circumstance thing. It's apparent in every collection.'

For the 'Voodoo' collection Berardi fused religion with music. 'I liked the idea of voodoo. It's hot and passionate. I had been to Brazil and liked the idea of macumba, which is the Brazilian mixture of Catholicism and voodoo. I loved the idea of ritual, and people being totally engrossed in music. You fall into a trance – it reminded me of being in a club. Once I get on the dance floor I can dance all night, regardless of whatever is happening around me.' The Voodoo Bride summed up all the references. The model, Michelle Hicks, strode out into the flames of the Camden Roundhouse set wearing an ethereal, embroidered chiffon dress with a head-dress that looked like an altar piece – it was made from a halo of candles that dripped wax as she moved. 'It was inspired by Fellini's *Casanova* and Catholic ceremonies like the festival of Santa Lucia where you wear a crown of candles. There's a purity and innocence about it as well.'

VOODOO BRIDE
Autumn/winter 1997

With lights shining through her gossamer-fine skirt and candles burning on her crown, the ethereal Voodoo Bride – modelled by **Michelle Hicks** – was one of Berardi's most spine-tingling catwalk moments. 'Don't ask me what a Voodoo Bride is,' Berardi says, but his creation is undoubtedly tinged with the powerful imagery of Catholicism.

SWAROVSKI DENIM DRESS
Autumn/winter 1998

Berardi takes an everyday, workwear fabric – denim – and makes it into a must-have investment with the addition of a single band of pink Swarovski crystals. The influence of the street and New York clubland is never far away.

LEATHER TROUSER SUIT
Autumn/winter 1998

Against a West Side Story backdrop, Berardi's collection gave uptown dressing a downtown twist. Here he makes a streetwise leather trouser suit a little more couture with some metal beading and embroidery work.

STREET SCENES
Autumn/winter 1998

The leather suit (*left*), with its bright, geometric insets, was inspired by biker leathers. The orange suit and matching trilby (by milliner Stephen Jones) are given some serious Fifth Avenue attitude.

GRAFFITI DRESS
Autumn/winter 1998

Graffiti, a reflection of urban street life, crops up regularly on the Berardi catwalk. This collection was inspired by the streets of Berardi's favourite metropolis, New York.

GUITAR JACKET
Spring/summer 1998

Miniature guitars were commissioned specially for this jacket and pinned on like charms. Part of the 'Las Vegas' section of the collection, which also featured a Guitar Hat, the jacket is pure rock'n'roll.

Another key inspiration is music. 'I had a record player from six months old,' he recalls. 'Music was my passion. I became an expert from listening to the radio and watching *Top of the Pops*.' In Berardi's mind, music and fashion feed off one another. Whenever he is in New York he visits the Sunday night Latin House club Cafe Con Leche; one of its DJs, Lord G, has mixed music live for Berardi's shows. The Brixton Academy show was full of references to the club, with its Latino passion and sexy tango dresses.

Film, too, has been another strong influence on Berardi's work. 'As kids we all loved movies. I had a particular passion for silent pictures.' The starting point to the collection for spring/summer 1999 was an obscure 1950s movie, *The Student Prince*, which Berardi recalled seeing as a teenager. For the autumn/winter 1999 collection, 'Never Mind the Borgias', Berardi worked directly with Fellini's costume-maker. 'When I was talking about the collection with Stephen [Jones] and Simon Costin, the set designer, they both mentioned *Fellini's Roma*, quite independently. So I watched it and there is one costume that lights up. So I got on the phone to Alfie in Italy and said I needed clothes that would light up, and described the outfit. In the film it was too stiff and I needed it to work on clothes, but I wanted the idea.'

43

FLASHING
CRUCIFIX COAT
Autumn/winter 1999

In typical Berardi fashion,
the outfit combines the
medieval (one reference
was Lucrezia Borgia) and
the religious. Berardi
commissioned Fellini's
costume designer to create
the dramatic light panel for
the coat.

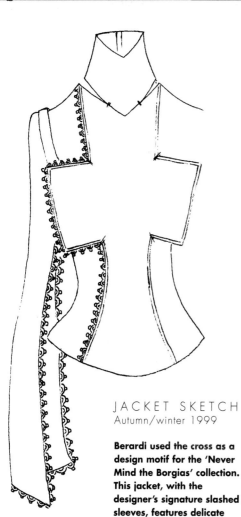

JACKET SKETCH
Autumn/winter 1999

Berardi used the cross as a design motif for the 'Never Mind the Borgias' collection. This jacket, with the designer's signature slashed sleeves, features delicate laser-cut edges, formerly a feature on his leather.

STUDDED DENIM
Autumn/winter 1999

Erin O'Connor wears Berardi's punk armour. The sleeves unzip at the elbow, and the trousers – which are seriously heavy – are studded all the way down. Punk and medieval references are cleverly fused in one outfit.

FASHION SUCKS
Autumn/winter 1999

The newsprint letters were cut out and pinned onto the outfit minutes before it went out on the catwalk. Berardi felt that the punk movement had been one of the most important of his lifetime, and wanted to use it in his final collection of the millennium.

In terms of clarity of vision, the autumn/ winter 1999 collection was a turning point. 'In the past I've probably been a bit lazy: we've taken ideas from all these disparate things and I've said, "Yes, put that in because I really like it." I've never been so succinct in a collection as I have in this one.' The starting point was red wine. 'I began thinking of collecting wine and how you can buy a two-hundred-year-old bottle and never open it, never taste it. The idea of it might set your tastebuds racing, but inside it could be vinegar, it might be hideous.' Typically for Berardi, he then began thinking, If the bottle of wine were a woman, who would it be? 'It had to be Lucrezia Borgia, because her image belied what she really was.' He was also, perhaps inevitably, affected by the collection being his last of the millennium. 'I looked at all the most significant things during my lifetime, and punk was probably one of the most important movements.' So he made his modern-day Lucrezia into a punk. However many references and inspirations there are behind a collection, it is important to Berardi that they fuse together in his own particular melting pot.

PUNK LUCREZIA
Autumn/winter 1999

Berardi based this collection around Lucrezia Borgia, the notorious Italian aristocrat associated with much 16th-century scandal but who ended her life as a nun. He used tartan (*left*) because of its connection with 1970s punks. The hooded toggle jacket (*right*) is designed to look sporty yet sinister.

**Inspired by punk and
bondage, Berardi made a
design feature of zips. The
multiple zips in this high-
neck collar can be undone
to change its shape.**

HAIR AND
MAKE-UP
Autumn/winter 1999

**Sharon Dowsett's eye make-
up was designed to make
the models look hard and
evil, while Nicholas
Jurnjack's extraordinary
hairpieces recall medieval
paintings. The model is
Kirsty Hume.**

47

Putting on a show

FASHION RUNS in never-ending cycles. As soon as one show is over and the collection under scrutiny with press and buyers, Antonio Berardi moves on to the next one, focusing on new research and development. All Berardi needs is a starting point: from there he will allow his mind to wander, taking in many other references along the way, however loosely they might be related.

The original inspiration for the spring/ summer 1999 collection is an obscure 1950s movie, *The Student Prince*, the story of a young Indian

aristocrat who is brought up by women. Stills from the film are tracked down from the British Film Institute library, and Warren Noronha, Berardi's London assistant, is dispatched to the British Library to find out all he can about Rajput princes and military uniforms. The themes for the collection include fencing, sailors, 'pretty pretty' and African warriors. 'The research period is never over until everything is in production,' says Berardi. 'Even then there might be last-minute ideas and changes to make.' (Less than a month before the show, for instance, Berardi decided he wanted wooden bangles. Noronha had two days to research bangle shapes and faxed his research to Italy where a suitable craftsman was found and research turned into reality.)

While research is underway, Berardi is busy with his Italian assistant, Alfie, sourcing the techniques and appropriate crafts that he wants to use. He begins to sketch his ideas. He might take a collar from a Rajput uniform or a seam detail from a fencing jacket and from that he will draw a dress or a jacket. A collection can consist of up to 120 outfits, although it will be edited down to a maximum of 60 for the show. The rest will be more commercial pieces, purely for selling.

Metro Studios, London, September 1998. The days before a show are times of intense planning and list-making. Berardi and stylist Sophia Neophitou work on casting and planning the running order, while the designer gives a sneak preview of the collection.

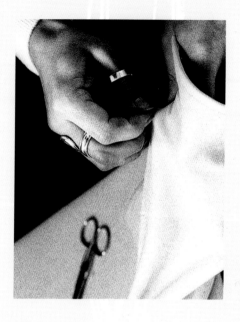
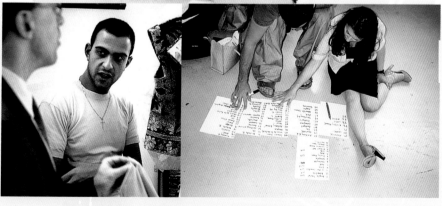

Designer and stylist make sure a wicker bodice and skirt fit a model and that the two work as a single outfit. These pieces are not intended for production but will ensure news pictures and demonstrate an idea or a particular technique.

While the collection starts coming to life, the search for a venue begins. For 'The Student Prince', to be shown in September, the hunt begins in May. St Pancras Hotel at King's Cross is a strong contender until fire regulations reveal that it will not hold everyone they want to invite. The Royal Horticultural Halls in Victoria is finally agreed upon and booked. Show producers, set builders and lighting designers are consulted.

By July it is time to talk to the hair and make-up designers, in this case the French hairstylist, Nicholas Jurnjack, and the British make-up artist, Sharon Dowsett. They are briefed on the themes of the show and discuss ideas with Berardi and his creative director, Sophia Neophitou. Jurnjack sketches an idea to create elaborate hairpieces – like hats made of hair – that he will bring with him on the day and blend in with the models' own hair.

The making of a show is the sum total of many parts. Clothes, set, lighting, music, hair, make-up and, of course, models: all have to come together at the same time. Logistics are complex. Two days before the show, the clothes arrive from Italy. A photographic studio in East London is booked for the final styling of the collection. The gold shoes arrive from Manolo Blahnik's Chelsea

The team decides on their next move during a fitting. Berardi's Italian-based assistant, Alfredo, is on hand for any suggestions. Berardi unpacks the shoes and accessories as the collection arrives by van from Italy. Jodie Kidd tries on one of the precious gold shoes.

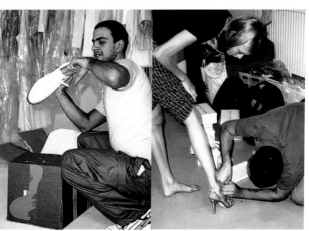

Models arrive, have their fittings and
leave within the space of ten minutes.
It is now that the outfits are styled,
accessorized and edited down to
around 60 outfits. Many more
clothes will be available to view when
buyers make their appointments to
order the collection.

studio, and all the other accessories, including the wicker corset and skirt, are laid out in preparation. Berardi trusts Neophitou to put the right outfit with the right accessories on the right model.

Models begin to be confirmed in the week before the show but it is not until they actually arrive for their fittings, the day before or even the day of the show, that their presence on the night is assured. On the afternoon of the show, the model Erin O'Connor arrives for her fitting. 'Look at her. She looks fabulous,' enthuses Berardi as she tries on her first outfit, a white fencing jacket and skin-tight stretch trousers. A polaroid is taken for the dressers to refer to during the show. The models like to do Berardi shows because they know they will be made to look like goddesses. They will have a completely new look with dramatic hair and make-up and it gives them the chance to work to their full capacity.

The DJ, Lord G, is now playing the final mix loud in the studio. He has flown over from New York specially for the show. 'It kills me,' says Berardi, as excited about the music as he is about the clothes. Lord G and Berardi had met a month earlier and talked through the collection's moods. Berardi's brief: 'Imagine you're in a fencing school: it's clean and very white.'

Agricultural Halls, London, 25 September 1998. Lord G, just arrived from New York, mixes the tracks he has discussed with Berardi. Backstage, meanwhile Nicholas Jurnjack pins up the models' hair into tiny, sleek buns, in preparation for his extraordinary lacquered hairpieces. Before the show the girls' hair will be sprayed jet black to blend seamlessly with the extensions.

Accessories are laid out ready to be put with the right outfit. The shoes are all designed by Manolo Blahnik; the famous 18-carat gold sandals are kept safely in their boxes until they are needed. The wooden bangles and wicker outfits were constructed by tradititional craftsmen in Italy. Most of the accessories will never go into production; they are purely for the catwalk show.

55

The final sound check before the show. All the elements are now in place.

Berardi and the team drive to the venue, with the clothes, about three hours before the show is due to begin. Nicholas Jurnjack is there, unpacking his extraordinary hairpieces, and the models begin to turn up. All the elements are all finally coming together. As the celebrities arrive front of house – Posh Spice and David Beckham along with various music people – the models get into their first outfits. And finally, the moment of truth: the show begins and Berardi stares into the TV monitor, transfixed.

The next day, Berardi looks at the newspaper reviews and the selling of the collection begins in earnest. But his mind is already elsewhere. 'The Student Prince' is old news. Already, he is thinking Lucrezia Borgia, dusty wine cellars and another city altogether: Milan.

At last: the 30-minute catwalk presentation. The show is a hit. Berardi celebrates backstage with hat designer Stephen Jones; models, friends and family join the party.

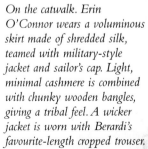

On the catwalk. Erin O'Connor wears a voluminous skirt made of shredded silk, teamed with military-style jacket and sailor's cap. Light, minimal cashmere is combined with chunky wooden bangles, giving a tribal feel. A wicker jacket is worn with Berardi's favourite-length cropped trouser.

The 'Student Prince' show featured Berardi's first foray into menswear. The all-white outfits were influenced by naval uniforms and fencing clothes. Left: Jodie Kidd gathers up her voluminous shredded silk skirt to walk down the runway.

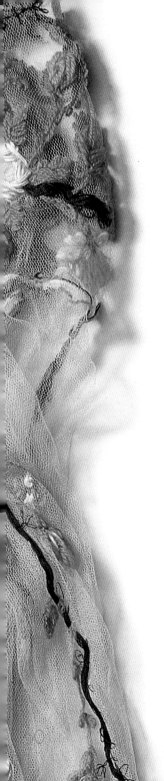

Chronology

1968
Antonio Berardi born in Grantham, Lincolnshire. His father runs an ice cream company. He and his four brothers and sisters are first-generation Italians; their parents moved to the UK from Sicily in the 1950s.

1990
Berardi is given an opportunity for work experience in London with John Galliano. Shortly afterwards wins a place on the Fashion BA degree course at Central St Martin's School of Art (his third attempt). Begins the course in September, whilst continuing at Galliano's part-time.

1992
Moves to France with the Galliano team, taking a year out from studies at St Martin's.

1994
Graduates from St Martin's. His final year collection – with shoes by Manolo Blahnik and vials of Berardi perfume for the press – causes a stir. The collection is bought by Liberty and A La Mode. Berardi wins a contract worth £20,000 to design a high street collection for Japan. The contract helps him finance his own business.

1995
The first catwalk show, for spring/summer 1996, is presented at Six Hamilton Place, Mayfair. Models include Stella Tennant and Kylie Minogue. Liberty and A La Mode buy for a second season. Kylie becomes known as a Berardi Girl.

1996
The second catwalk show is held in February at the East Tent Lawn, outside the Natural History Museum. The third show, for spring/summer 1997, is held in September in the Crush Bar at the Royal Opera House, Covent Garden. It is the 'must-see' show of the season. In December Berardi signs up with Italian manufacturers, Givuesse, who take care of the production and manufacturing side of the Berardi label.

1997

The autumn/winter 1997 collection is shown at the Camden Roundhouse; the theme is 'Voodoo'. The collection sells to over 55 stockists worldwide. Prince comes to watch the show and Berardi is confirmed as a star name on the international fashion map. Berardi is appointed consultant for the leather and suede manufacturers, Ruffo; the deal lasts for one season. The spring/summer 1998 collection is shown at Brixton Academy. Lord G is flown over from New York to mix the soundtrack live; Demi Moore attends. Stockists reach over one hundred worldwide. Berardi is nominated best new designer for the VH1 Awards in New York, alongside Narciso Rodriguez. The spring/summer 1998 collection in shown in New York as part of the MTV 'Fashionably Loud' extravaganza.

1998

The autumn/winter 1998 collection is shown at the Combustion Chambers, a circus rehearsal space in Hoxton Square, East London. The entire collection is later stolen from outside Berardi's studio; the thieves are never caught. The spring/summer 1999 collection is shown at the Agricultural Halls, near Victoria. The theme is 'The Student Prince', after the 1950s movie. Posh Spice and David Beckham watch from the front row.

1999

Berardi is nominated for British Fashion Designer of the Year 1999, alongside Clements Ribeiro and Hussein Chalayan. Makes his debut at Milan Fashion Week with the 'Never Mind the Borgias' collection for autumn/winter 1999.

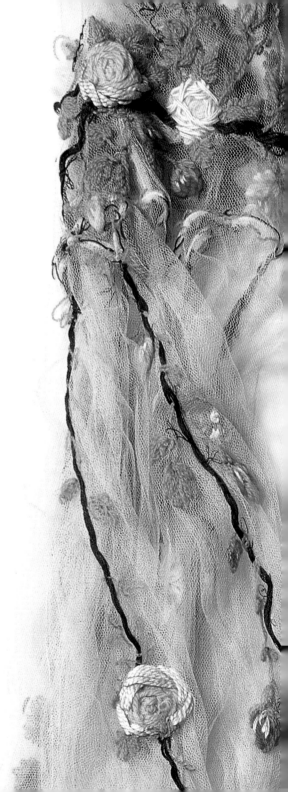

Index

Acknowledgements

The publishers wish to thank Antonio Berardi, Jasbir Uppal and all at the Antonio Berardi studio for their kind assistance with all aspects of this book. Thanks also to Sandro Sodano for the 'Student Prince' photographic shoot, and to Stephen Jones for permission to use the sketches on page 29.

Photographic credits
All photographs by Chris Moore, with the following exceptions:

Offida Tourism Office: page 26 top and bottom left.

Guy Ryecart: pages 13 right, 18 far left (*detail*), 21 left and middle, 22 left and middle, 28 bottom, 30 bottom right, 32 left, 34 left, 35 top and bottom left and middle, 38–39, 40 left and middle, 43.

Sandro Sodano: pages 5, 6, 28 top, 48–57, 60 far left.